Serial

HOMICIDE

(Book 3)

Notorious Serial Killers Series

Australian Serial Killers

by: RJ PARKER

"This is a work of nonfiction. No names have been changed, no characters invented, no events fabricated."

– RJ Parker Publishing

Serial

HOMICIDE

(Book 3)

Notorious Serial Killers Series

Australian Serial Killers

by: RJ PARKER

ISBN-13: 9781987902211
ISBN-10: 1987902211

Copyright and Published (01.2017)

by RJ Parker Publishing, Inc.

Published in United States of America

Copyrights

Table of Contents

AUDIOBOOKS at RJ Parker Publishing
http://rjpp.ca/ASTORE-AUDIOBOOKS

Our collection of **CRIMES CANADA** books on
Amazon.
http://bit.ly/ASTORE-CRIMESCANADA

TRUE CRIME Books by RJ Parker Publishing on
Amazon.
http://rjpp.ca/ASTORE-TRUECRIME

ACTION / FICTION Books by Bernard DeLeo on
Amazon.
http://bit.ly/ACTION-FICTION

1. The Backpacker Murders

Background

Serial killers are often associated with the perpetration of willful murder. The Australian Criminal Code defines willful murder as the intentional, unlawful killing of another person. In murder cases, it is the prosecutor's duty to prove the accused guilty. This means that the prosecutor on a given case must prove one's guilt beyond reasonable doubt. The definition given with regard to murder by the statute also includes intentional killing of another person.

In murder cases, sentencing of the convicted murderer usually happens upon the proving of guilt. Sentencing of the perpetrators of crimes is regarded as a legal sanction for the crimes done. One type of sanctions that may be imposed on a convicted murderer is the natural life sentencing. However, this type of sanction may be considered inhumane.

Murders

The famous notorious backpacker murders that were allegedly committed by Ivan Milat involved the killing of seven backpackers that included Deborah Everist and James Gibson who lived in Victoria, Caroline Clarke and Joanne Walters who resided in the United Kingdom, and Anja Habscheid, Simone Schmidl and Gabor Neugebeuer who were all German nationals.

All the seven victims were aged between nineteen and twenty-two years. When they met their untimely death, they were travelling to Sydney and hitchhiking south in order to attend a musical festival named Confest, near Albury. This was mentioned by one of the victim's mother in a subsequent interview in 2006. The victims were murdered and buried in the Belango State Forest where they were discovered between September 1992 and November 1993 after they had gone missing between December 1989 and April 1992. At the time of discovery, the victims' bodies were considerably decomposed.

All the victims had the signs of brutal attacks, ranging from decapitation, multiple gunshot wounds in their heads, stab wounds, strangulation, to spinal cord severing. These were determined by the forensic team that was involved in conducting the forensic study of the case. Moreover, the forensic report ascertained that all the victims except one had been sexually abused either prior to their deaths or after killing them.

The accused person in this series of inhumane killings, Ivan Robert Marko Milat, was born in 1947 in Guildford, Australia. He came from a Yugoslavian migrant family as one of their fourteen children. Ivan Milat started being constantly in conflict with the law from his early age. Before the Backpackers series of murders, Milat had been acquitted from a couple of alleged rape cases in 1971 for the lack of convincing evidence against him.

Capture

After discovering the first and second set of decomposing bodies which belonged to the backpackers, questions were raised by all concerned persons, including the Australians and the international community at large. Meanwhile, what had first appeared as an

9

isolated crime started to be considered in a new light; the possible thorough work of a serial killer prompted the Australian police department to launch serious investigations with the aim of catching the perpetrator or perpetrators of the crimes.

However, even after conducting investigations through numerous public informants, no convincing information with regard to a possible suspect was obtained. It only happened when a survived victim of Ivan Milat went to the police and provided more information about him.

The surviving victim, named Paul Onions, was very helpful in positively detailing the accused's physical appearance that later helped in identifying Ivan Milat. Paul Onions had previously sought the help of the police in 1990 when the accused had offered him a lift in his car identifying himself as Bill, along the road where the remains of the seven backpackers were discovered later. Onions narrowly escaped after Milat threatened him with a gun which caused him to flee from the vehicle leaving his possessions and travelling documents behind. He took a lift from a lady after encountering Milat on that day. Onions came from the UK and was searching for a job in Australia at that time.

Following the incident, Onions returned home to the United Kingdom. During the incidents of the backpackers murders, he came forward and described his encounter with Milat. His 1990 details were corroborated by the lady who had offered him a lift. It was this fact that eventually gave the police a legal opportunity to apprehend Ivan Milat.

Following his apprehension by the police, some belongings of the victims, such as their clothing were recovered in his house and also his mother's house where he had been living at the time when the backpackers incident occurred. The investigators also identified the weapons used by the murderer. A shirt that Onions described as a part of the property he had left in Milat's vehicle upon fleeing was also among the items that were recovered in his mother's house, further corroborating the facts given by Onions.

In 1994, Ivan Milat and his brother Walter were arrested with a .22 caliber firearm. It was similar to the one which was used in inflicting multiple gunshot wounds on the victims' bodies. Initially Milat was arrested on account of robbery but later his arrest details were amended to include seven counts of murder.

Trial and Sentencing

Upon his arrest, Ivan Milat was charged with robbery and possession of a weapon on May 23, 1994, and brought before the trial court for entering a plea of guilty. The charges, however, were amended to include seven counts of murder by May 30, 1994. The accused kept saying that he is not guilty even after being charged for the murders. The prosecutor was called on to present his case, a task which took twelve weeks. Within this time, the prosecutor presented various pieces of evidence to incriminate him.

The only alleged victim of Ivan Milat, Paul Onions, was called upon by the prosecutor, and then he gave his testimony of the unnerving events of 1990. Paul Onions was a key witness in this series of murder charges and he was the one who identified the murder suspect. The members of the Milat family also acted as witnesses and presented the court with their testimonies. Moreover, the forensic team was called upon to give their expert opinions. A DNA profiling specialist indicated that a cloth that was retrieved from the accused's garage had blood which matched the DNA of one of the murder victims, Caroline Clarke. The court was presented with photos of the seven victims who were buried in shallow graves by the murderer.

Once the prosecution case was closed, Ivan Milat's defense team was called upon to present its case. Milat denied all the accusations that were brought against him. The accused tried to poke holes in the prosecutor's evidence without any gains for the next three weeks following the prosecutor's presentation.

When both sides had presented their side of the case, the jury found Ivan Milat guilty in all seven counts of murder although Justice Hunt claimed that it is almost impossible for a sole person to commit all the seven backpack murders. A conviction judgment was read by Chief Justice David Hunt who was presiding over the case. The accused was sentenced to serve six years imprisonment for attacking Paul Onions and seven consecutive life imprisonments for the seven murders. The judgment was enacted in 1996 and Ivan Milat was sent to incarceration in Goulburn Prison under maximum security surveillance.

The Appeal Case

Following Ivan Milat's conviction by the Court of First Instance, he appealed against the decision in 1996. The appeal was lodged in the Supreme Court of New South Wales Court of Criminal Appeals. Ivan Milat, the appellant, sought a declaratory order that Justice David Hunt, the presiding trial judge, had made a mistake by admitting photographic identification as the method to identify him as Paul Onion's attacker. He also asked the court to look into the possibility that the trial jury had been influenced by the media and rendered the decision against him.

The hearing of the appeal was scheduled for November, 4, 1996, and the appellant notified the Court of Appeal that he would be representing himself before it. For determining the first issue with regard to the photographic identification, the Court of Criminal Appeals examined the evidence that was used in identifying the appellant. In the trial court, the appellant was positively identified by Paul Onions among thirteen photographs of suspects that were presented to him. The witness then identified Ivan through the distinctive moustache that he wore at the time while he attacked Onions.

Ivan's identification through the moustache was further corroborated by a photograph that he took wearing the same moustache. The appellant disputed the identification method used by informing the court that Onion's original description of him varied from his true appearance. Onions had described him as being in his thirties while in fact he was forty-six at the time the original identification was conducted.

The appellant claimed that the identification proceedings were not videotaped. He stated that the jury made an 'unforgivable mistake' for having been partly informed by the method of identification used to identify him by Onions.

The Court of Criminal Appeals mentioned that the Court of First Instance did not err by admitting the photograph as evidence through which the appellant was identified by Paul Onions, and dismissed his first submission. The Court of Criminal Appeals also stated that the evidence which was presented before the trial court by the prosecutor to identify the appellant was undisputedly corroborated by the evidence that helped identify the appellant. The Appellate Court concluded that Honorable Justice David Hunt was not unfair in accepting photographic evidence as a form of identifying the appellant.

Ivan argued that due to comments the prosecutor had made and were publicized, the jury was influenced by the public opinion and the media. Considering this possibility, the court acknowledged the fact that the case had attracted global attention. During the trial, some comments that the prosecutor made were also presented to the public domain. The case undoubtedly attracted a lot of publicity. Due to these reasons, the appellant claimed that the trial was conducted unfairly because of the emotions the case elicited from the public.

The appellant further argued that some witnesses were influenced by the publicity of some of his photos which were published in the 'Who' Magazine, thus resulting in unfair justice. The release of these photos caused the 'Who' Magazine to get sued on the ground of contempt of court. In this case, the trial court stated that publication of the appellant's photographs could affect the administration of justice. However, the court stated that such publication did not influence the justice administration in this case in any manner.

All the presiding judges in the Court of Criminal Appeal agreed that they were satisfied beyond any reasonable doubt that the trial had been conducted fairly and was justly decided by the trial jury. The case was dismissed by the court.

Appealing in the High Court of Australia

In 2004, Ivan Milat filed an appeal to the High Court of Australia appealing his conviction.

However, an application for special leave to lodge an appeal in this case was denied by the three high court judges who were determining the application. Upon denying the applicant's plea, Justice Gummow stated that the Court of Criminal Appeals had decided the matter rightly. Furthermore, the judge went ahead to state that the time stipulated under the statute with regard to applications for appeal in the High Court of Australia had expired long ago.

Appealing in the Supreme Court of the New South Wales

The dismissal of Milat's application for special leave to file an appeal in the High Court of Australia compelled him to appeal in the Supreme Court of New South Wales in 2005. The appeal inquired about Milat's multiple life sentence convictions. The application submitted argued that Milat's conviction was unfair, since the trial court had raised doubts as to whether or not he was an alleged sole perpetrator in the famous 'Backpack' murders of the early 1990s.

In a written submission of fifty pages, Milat's application for an inquiry on his conviction demanded further evidence that was made against his motor vehicle. The applicant mentioned that the court was misled by the testimonies of Paul Onions and Mrs. Berry (the lady who gave Onions a lift after he was attacked by Ivan Milat) when they described the features used to identify his vehicle. However, it was concluded that Ivan Milat was convicted beyond any reasonable doubt that he was the attacker of Paul Onions.

The application for inquiry regarding the conviction of Ivan Milat was dismissed. The court interpreted Section 474D and said that once a person was convicted either at the trial stage or at the appellate courts and such a person subsequently used all the appeal avenues available to him, the provision of Section 474D could not be construed to such a person with a new avenue of appeal. The Supreme Court of New South Wales stated that the ground for appeal had already been dealt with at the trial court and at the subsequent appeal stage of the case. It was concluded that submissions before the court did not raise any doubt about the applicant's guilt.

In 2006, Milat made another application under Section 78 raising the question on adducible evidence before the court of law upon which his ground on the application for appeal was based. The application was made to inquire about his conviction and sentencing. Similarly, the application was set aside on the ground that it did not raise any doubt about whether he was not guilty.

In 2008, Ivan Milat made a third application to the New South Wales Supreme Court regarding the inquiry of his conviction which was seeking a declaration that the Crown Court was wrong in convicting him under Section 474D of the Crimes Act of 1900. However, the application in this case was treated as being made under Section 78 of the Repealed Act. In this application, he argued that since the Crown Court could not determine whether the Backpacker murders were committed by a single person, it did not have to convict him.

Chief Justice McClellan stated that the trial court was only tasked with the duty of determining whether or not the appellant was guilty but not whether other persons were involved, a duty that was well executed. The application was dismissed for lack of raising any doubt about the applicant's guilt.

In 2010, Milat made his fourth application for inquiring about his conviction and sentencing by the Crown Court. In this application, handwritten submissions were made raising several issues: his concern about the reliability of the trial court's primary evidence, the existence of the new pieces of evidence, submission that the DNA evidence did not implicate the applicant in the series of murders and that he had an alibi. The Court stated that there were no special facts that justified further action and thus dismissed the application.

His 2010 application was followed by a similar application in 2014 that was subsequently denied. In 2015, he made his sixth application to the same court for the inquiry of his conviction and sentencing. The application was brought pursuant to the provisions of Section 78 of the repealed Crimes (Appeal and Review) Act of 2001. The application was dismissed on the ground that it was a repetition of the previous five applications.

Conclusion

Backpacker murders were committed by 71-year-old Ivan Robert Marko Milat who was 46 at the time of his arrest. He was solely convicted and sentenced for seven consecutive life imprisonments under maximum security surveillance. His conviction was upheld although the court was dubious about the possibility of him solely committing the murders of his seven victims. During his trial, DNA evidence had only ensured the high probability of the involvement of one or more of Milat's family members in perpetrating the crimes, but it was not clearly established who among Milat's family members had committed the murders.

2. Arnold Karl Sodeman

Background

Arnold Sodeman, better known as the "school girl strangler", was born in Victoria in 1899. He grew up witnessing his mother suffering from bouts of amnesia. His family had a long history of mental instability. Arnold`s father was mentally ill and sent to a mental institution. It was said that his grandfather also died in a mental institution. It was obvious that Arnold had a disturbed childhood. It was this unstable childhood that later influenced part of his decisions as a grown man. When he was 18 years old, he was sent to prison for reforms after he was found guilty of larceny. This didn't seem to have any positive impact on his character because, shortly after he was released from prison, he was found guilty of armed robbery and charged for it. He wounded a railway station master this time. He was sentenced for three years with hard labor. You would be wrong if you think that he learned his lesson because, apparently, he did not serve his sentence. He later escaped from the prison but got caught again. Thus his sentence was extended to a further 12 months in prison with hard labor. This caused him to serve four years in prison for his crimes.

After being released from the prison, he tried to turn over a new leaf. He decided to get himself a job as a laborer in Melbourne. He later moved to Gibson and worked as a laborer. For some time, things started to look up for him. His future looked bright and he even decided to get married to his sweetheart Bernice Pope. In 1928, Bernice gave birth to their daughter Joan.

They seemed to be a happy little family although Sodeman used to suffer from depression occasionally. He became addicted to alcohol and used to constantly get drunk in order to get rid of his frustrations in life. Although he drank heavily, he never raised a finger to harm his family. He wasn't violent towards his wife and daughter. On the contrary, he was known to be a hard-working man and he was even described as admirable by society. People observed him as being generous and a law-abiding citizen, a character that would drastically change for the worse.

The Chain of Murders

On November 9, 1930, he did something that caught everyone by surprise. He abducted Mena Griffiths, a 12-year-old school girl who was playing with her friends at a local playground. He managed to trick Mena`s friends by giving them some money to get some ice cream. While her friends went to get the ice cream, Sodeman told Mena that he wanted her to do something for him. In her innocence, Mena agreed to help him, and by the time her friends came back, she had already left with Sodeman. Then Mena`s body was recovered two days later at Ormond. This 12-year-old girl's bound, gagged and strangled body was found in an abandoned building.

Sodeman's gruesome hobby did not end with Mena's event. He abducted a 16-year-old girl called Hazel Wilson on January 10, 1931. Hazel's body was later found in a suburb in Ormond; she was strangled to death. Similarly, both girls had their hands bound behind their backs using pieces of their clothing. Though the cases were under investigation by the police, no evidence led them towards suspecting Sodeman. There was no witness of the murders and, therefore, no leads to aid the police in their investigation. It seemed like Sodeman had gotten away with the murders.

On January 1, 1935, when everyone was welcoming the New Year, Sodeman made his third strike. This was quickly becoming a habit with him. While at Inverloch, he abducted a 12-year-old girl named Ethel Belshaw when she went out to buy ice cream. Just like his previous murders, he strangled her to death and dumped her body.

By now, the killings had started taking their toll on the people. However, Sodeman had developed a thirst for taking more lives and on December 1, 1935, he struck again, taking the life of another victim. This time, it was a 6-year-old girl named June Rushmer who was his fourth victim. June Rushmer was on her way home from the park when she met Sodeman. And like the other girls, it did not take long for Sodeman to abduct and kill her. Just one day after her abduction, her lifeless body was found less than 2 kilometers away from Leongatha where she lived. Like all his previous victims, June's body was also found bound, strangled and gagged. It became evident that Sodeman had made this his signature way of killing. It is, however, not clear if the police had picked up this trend and could relate the murders to the same person. Her abduction was witnessed by some people who claimed to have seen June with a man on a bicycle before she was reported missing. This would later be the basis of investigations carried out by the police and possibly the only way to stop the murders.

Ironically, Sodeman used to work as part of a crew that repaired roadways at that time. No one would ever think that he was responsible for any of the murders. His character as a person was the complete opposite of what one would expect to find on a murderer. One morning while on a tea break, one of Sodeman's workmates jokingly stated that he saw Sodeman on a bike where June went missing. Sodeman's response shocked his workmates. He burst out in anger saying that he hadn't been anywhere near the crime scene. This caught the workmates by surprise because they had never witnessed Sodeman being that angry. It was unlike him to respond in such a manner. This raised their suspicions and they decided to report the matter to the police.

The Capture of Arnold K. Sodeman

Upon receiving this news, the police rushed to Sodeman's workplace and quickly arrested him. What surprised even the police was that as soon as they took Sodeman in for questioning, he confessed to all the killings. The police didn't expect this, and at first they weren't sure whether to believe what Sodeman was saying. This prompted them to ask Sodeman more questions related to the murders. His attention to detail in explaining what had happened compelled the police to look at the matter differently. They started believing that he could have committed the murders. Sodeman explained everything in a way that only someone who was present during the murders would know. He described how he choked his victims by linking his thumbs to make the process easier. His statements were extremely detailed, and he was sure not to leave out anything that happened during the murders. This stunned the police, since they could not understand why Sodeman would commit such crimes and later confess without trying to hide anything. Though these questions did not provide any logical answers to them, they proceeded with his arrest and he was later presented to face trial.

Sodeman's Trial

After Sodeman`s arrest and subsequent confession to the murders that he committed, an inquest was made on June Rushmer`s case. The case of this 6-year-old girl who was abducted and found strangled to death was resumed. Sodeman, now a 36-year-old man, attended the court session. Dr Mollison, the then government pathologist, confirmed that June`s hands were tied behind her back using a piece of cloth. Her body was found with a blood-stained cloth forced inside her mouth. Her neck was tied using a piece of sock that was torn. Her body was full of bruises, and Dr Mollison concluded that her death was caused by suffocation.

June`s friend, Nancy Viola, confirmed that on December 1, she was at the Leongatha reserve playing with June. She said that at around 7:15 pm, June left and was no longer at the park. They looked around for her but could not find her.

William Henry Money claimed that he

saw Sodeman riding his bicycle towards the reserve. He also added that Sodeman had a strange look while he stared at him and that he did not speak to him. William said that he found that reaction peculiar. However, he brushed off the thought and went about his business.

The second witness, Vincent Desmond Ryan, who also lived in Leongatha, stated that though he was 90 yards away and therefore couldn't confirm beyond reasonable doubt to have seen Sodeman, he saw a man riding a bike with a little girl seated on the front. This took place between 7:15 pm and 7:30 pm the same evening when William Henry Money had met up with Sodeman.

A senior Detective known as O`Keefe confirmed that Sodeman talked to one of his officers. The officer known as Delminico asked Sodeman if he wanted to make a confession regarding June`s death. Delminico offered to excuse himself from the room in order to allow Sodeman to make his statement. Sodeman replied that he could stay and listen to his confessions. He acknowledged that there was more than one murder, meaning June`s death wasn't the only one. Then he proceeded with his statement.

In his statement, Sodeman stated that

while riding his bike, he came across June Rushmer who was walking on the footpath next to the tennis court and heading home. He claimed that when June saw him riding his bike, she asked if he could give her a lift, and since they both knew each other, he decided to give her a ride on his bicycle. He went ahead to explain how he rode down the path and made a turn on the road that led to the sanitary depot. He said that when June noticed that the corner was about 100 yards away, she said that she would be okay from there on. Sodeman claimed to have gotten off his bike and told June that it was okay for her to walk the remaining distance. He said that he then ran after June and she ran into the bush after being scared. What happened afterwards would then shock many as Sodeman explained how he ran into the bush after June and strangled her using his bare hands. By now, everyone in the room could not believe what they were hearing. He explained without leaving out any details regarding how June screamed and later became limp. Sodeman later removed June's bloomers and jammed them into her mouth. He used a belt from June`s frock to tie across the bloomers around the back of June`s neck. After explaining the turn of events, the coroner asked that Sodeman be held for trial.

Sodeman was found guilty in February 1936, after a trial that lasted for two days. The jury found Sodeman guilty of taking the life of June Rushmer, and the judge later gave him a death sentence.

Judge Charles Gavan Duffy told the Jury to consider the opinions of expert medical witnesses on issues relating to June`s body. He said that the opinions from the medical witnesses could be proved through surgery. He also asked them to consider the medical witnesses' opinions regarding the possibility of Sodeman suffering from a mental disorder. But Sodeman's plea of insanity was rejected by the jury.

Dr. A. J. Philpott, who was the government medic, together with his assistant, Dr. R.T Allan, and Dr. Reginald Ellery who practiced as a psychiatrist, gave supporting evidence that Sodeman actually had a psychological disorder that caused him to experience obsessional impulses that he couldn't control when under the influence of alcohol. The doctors' argument was that Sodeman was insane while committing the murders because, regarding his state of mind and the fact that he was intoxicated when the murders happened, they felt that Sodeman could not control his actions. They also mentioned the the fact that

Sodeman's father and grandfather both died insane and Sodeman's condition could be related to his family history and was probably genetic.

Appeals

In April 24, 1936, a statement was extracted from the local daily newspaper which mentioned that the English King's counsel would be pleading in Arnold Sodeman's case before the Judicial Committee of the Privy Council. This is where Sodeman had been accused for the murder of June Rushmer. Mr. C. H. Auty, who stood as Sodeman's solicitor, said that he had sent a cable message to Mr. D. N. Pritt, the leading King's counsel. Mr. D.N Pritt, who was also a member of the House of Commons, was supposed to represent Sodeman during his absence. Sodeman requested for special leave which he had planned to use in order to appeal against the Australian High Court. But the Australian High court had previously refused to grant Sodeman special leave. Sodeman's plan was to use it for his appeal against the judgment passed on his case.

Mr. Auty sent a written request to Mr. Dunstan, the Premier, requesting the government to issue a reprieve for Sodeman until his application can be determined. Mr.

Auty stated that he was in the process of preparing a petition for the appeal of special leave. The documents were expected to be ready for dispatch to England the following week. He stated that the document that needs to be sent urgently to London was the affidavit that supported the application. They agreed that the affidavit could be signed by Sodeman before the expiry of his reprieve on May 4, which was the day of execution. They expected the executive commission to go ahead and grant them the reprieve. A report was then expected from the department of Crown Law the following week. The Cabinet then decided whether to grant the request upon which the Executive Council could take immediate action.

But the appeal made by Sodeman for the case filed against him was not successful. The appeal was filed on the grounds that the evidence admitted by the judge was gathered erroneously. This evidence included those submitted for Mena Griffiths', Hazel Wilson's and Ethel Belshaw's deaths. The appeal was also filed on the basis that the Jury was misdirected by the Judge on the plea of insanity and about the law and what it dictates about the relationship between drinking, insanity and manslaughter.

Execution

All this time, Sodeman didn't ask for a reprieve. He feared that if they spared his life, he would murder more people. He was more afraid of himself and his actions than facing death. The fact that he knew he couldn't control himself influenced him to die rather than to live with the anguish of what would happen if his life was spared. On the eve of Sodeman`s execution, he spent a lot of his time with Edward Cornelius playing draughts. Edward himself was waiting for a death sentence for the murder of a Reverend Cecil from Fitzroy. Before his execution, Sodeman told the Governor that he was glad that it was almost over.

On June 1, 1936, Arnold Karl Sodeman was hanged by the state. It happened at the Pentridge Prison in Coburg where his body was then buried. Before he was hanged, the Sheriff gave him an opportunity to speak and asked him if he had anything to say, but Sodeman declined the offer saying he had nothing to say. He seemed unmoved as he walked to the scaffold.

When an autopsy was done on Sodeman`s body, it was discovered that Sodeman had a degenerative disorder known as leptomenengitis. This disease caused serious congestion in Sodeman`s brain and the condition tended to worsen when he consumed alcohol.

On the 75th anniversary of the death of Ethel Belshaw, a Leongatha local daily newspaper published an interview with Sodeman`s former neighbor known as Maureen Lewis. Maureen was with Sodeman`s family in Inverloch on the day when Ethel Belshaw, the 12-year-old girl was brutally murdered by Sodeman. Maureen claimed that, in fact, she was the intended victim. When the Sodemans set off for a trip from Leongatha to go enjoy a day out as a family, Maureen had tagged along as she was a good friend of Sodemans' only daughter Joan, and they were neighbors as well. They had planned a fun-filled day out which also doubled up as a long play day for Joan and Maureen. Maureen said that if Sodeman`s wife had not stepped in to stop them from going for the ice cream, she would have been the one who would die that day. Ethel, the 12-year-old victim, was seen on the same day going to fetch some ice cream from a milk bar along the beach road in the town. On that New Year`s eve back in 1935, Sodeman had planned to take Maureen out for some ice cream. Bernice refused to let Sodeman take Maureen for ice cream unless Sodeman would agree to take his daughter Joan as well. This idea did not seem to please Sodeman, and therefore the trip to the ice cream parlor did not happen. When Maureen looked back at what happened to Ethel, she still could not believe that she would have been the one who would die on that day.

Many people in Leongatha, including Maureen attested to the fact that Sodeman did not seem quite normal to them. He always seemed aloof to people, and most kids in the area were afraid of him. Maureen also added that though Sodeman didn't seem quite normal to them, no one would dare to call him "Old Sodeman" as everyone feared being called up by their fathers and forced to refer him as Mr. Sodeman. However, he remained Old Sodeman to the kids since he used to wear sandshoes and they always found him creepy.

3. The Moorhouse Murders

Would you mind being the owner of the home to the 3 Moorhouse Street serial killers? The Moorhouse Street home has actually been listed on the market four times since 1998. The home of the serial killers is an integral part of the Moorhouse murders as it was the scene where most of the killings, raping and psychotic pleasure for the couple took place. David Birnie and his wife Catherine formed a team that inflicted great suffering and eventually murdered four women in their house in the southern suburbs of Perth in the year 1986.

David and Catherine used to read a certain book that gave them the blueprint of their plot for killing innocents after torture and rape. It is believed that the couple got their inspiration from the book and used it to make their dark, psychopathic sexual desires come true. Their criminal activities came into the spotlight only after a fifth victim managed to escape after she was abducted at knife point. This couple was then given a 20-year minimum sentence under very strict security.

How the serial killer couple came to be

The couple met during their childhood and grew up in a little rural town on the outskirts of Perth. Catherine's mom had already passed on while her husband was deeply buried in alcoholism. It is this sadistic existence that united the two to form a couple that would later on kill innocents in cold blood.

The couple was 35-years-old at the time of these crimes and found a uniting factor between them from their teenage lives. As teenagers the couple teamed up to commit various burglaries. After that, each went on their separate way. Birnie got married while Catherine worked as a house help. She ended up marrying the son of her boss and bore him seven children. Meanwhile, Birnie's marriage went into tatters. When Catherine and Birnie met again, they rekindled their affair. She left her husband and kids for Birnie.

Despite his mild scrawny look, David was a sexually insatiable man. He craved intercourse virtually all the time and wanted it at least six times a day. James was his 21-year-old brother who had been imprisoned with cases of sexual offense. He narrated to the press how the serial killer couple broke up temporarily in 1984 after David attempted to have intercourse with him by climbing into his bed while he was sleeping. For his 21st birthday, David allowed James to have intercourse with Catherine as his birthday present.

In the year 1985, Catherine and David had discussions about the idea of abducting girls and raping them. The murder of Mary Neilson, which was their first encounter seemed somewhat unplanned.

Thirty years have gone down the line since Catherine and David claimed the first victim of their atrocities, which also marked the start of the perverted Moorhouse murders.

Serial killings committed in a four-week span

The sadistic serial killers committed a total of four murders, and their fifth attempt was the one that led to their atrocities being put in the spotlight. They managed to pull off five incidences in a time span of four weeks. The following are the accounts of their murders.

October 6, 1986: Mary Neilson

Mary Neilson was the first victim of a series of other killings that followed later on. She was a 22-year-old psychology student who was also working on a part-time basis at a food outlet in Perth. She lived in an affluent suburb when she first met the serial killers. Neilson met with her fate when she was shopping for some low-priced car tires. She met Catherine and David to whom she gave her phone contact after they suggested that she visit their home to check out some tires they had.

Paul Kidd, the *Australia's Serial Killers* author, said that Mary had visited an auto spare parts shop where David was working after which he suggested that she come by his home. After their agreement, Mary showed up at his Moorhouse Street home in Willagee, Perth.

On arrival, she was pulled indoors by Catherine who held her at knife point before she was bound. It was on early October 6, 1986, in which she had a lecture in the course of the day. Mary decided to pass by the serial killers' home on her way to her lecture and that marked her demise.

Mary Neilson was the first victim for these killers, but they had planned for it. Nothing about the attack seemed random. David threw her on the bed while suffocating his victim with his scrawny body while raping her. Kidd said that Catherine was present during the act and sensually touched him to arouse his sadistic desires even more.

The couple loved the struggles by the 22-year-old woman trying to free herself. They tortured her even more before finally putting an end to her misery. The couple needed a way to drive away any suspicions. David drove their victim's car, then parked it close to a police station so that it would not raise any suspicions.

They threw Mary in his car and drove her to Glen Eagles National Park after which David raped her ruthlessly again. She was then stabbed in the chest, then a rope tightened on her neck. He used a shovel from the car's trunk to dig a shallow pit where she was buried. They believed that they had gotten away with the murder. Mary's death was only the start of a killing spree by the couple who had plans of replicating their crime again and again. They visualised a graveyard filled with bodies at the park. The couple spent weeks researching the best ways of committing murder and getting away with it.

October 20, 1986: Susannah Candy

Their lust for cold-blood murder grew faster, and two weeks later, they had Susannah Candy as their second victim. She was only 15 years old at the time of her abduction while hitch-hiking along Claremont's Stirling Highway in Perth.

It is said that Catherine was the one who was in charge of picking the victims, so she took note of Susannah. The Birnies offered to give her a ride, and as soon as they got hold of her, they tied her up and took her to their Moorhouse Street home.

David had planned to keep their second victim for some time before killing her. So he forced her to write two letters to her parents to inform them that she was fine. David forced her to even call them as well.

After settling the worries of her parents, David and Catherine had their victim tied on the bed, where they interchangeably raped and sodomised her. When they had their sadistic desires fulfilled by the teenager, David tried to strangle her, but Susannah fought hard for her life. When he couldn't accomplish it, he forcibly drugged her with sleeping pills, then asked Catherine to strangle the teen... as a sign of her love for him! Catherine was as crazy as David had imagined, so she did it. After her murder, Susannah's body was buried just next to Mary's, their initial victim.

They needed more victims to satisfy their sick sexual fantasies that were now growing apace. So they sought for their third victim. At that stage, they had also devised several clever methods of luring their victims, torturing and eventually murdering them, then covering up the crimes.

November 1, 1986: Noelene Patterson

The gap between their first and second murder was two weeks. The third murder, however, occurred after eleven days which showed that indeed their lust for these atrocities was strengthening. Noelene Patterson was 31 years old. She worked as a hostess and was a friend to the Birnies. They were actually pretty close friends. Catherine and David had even assisted her to repaint her house a couple of weeks earlier before she fell prey to their masochistic acts. Her car had run out of fuel

45

while driving home. So she stood beside the car awaiting an oncoming vehicle to hitch-hike.

Noelene was happy to see her friends when they pulled over. Catherine and David welcomed her and she was immediately held at knife-point. They drove her back to their home after which she was repeatedly raped. The Birnies had planned to kill Noelene once through with their sickening acts the same night. However, they imprisoned her for three more days.

This crime had a somewhat crazy twist in that David had started to develop feelings for their victim, and this perhaps was the reason for the long wait. Just as it is with many couples, Catherine became jealous and gave her significant other an ultimatum to kill Noelene, failure to which she would kill herself. He responded by forcing sleeping pills into Noelene's mouth, then strangled her while she was asleep. Her body was as well buried along with the other victims.

November 5, 1986: Denise Brown

Four days after Noelene's death, the Birnies continued their ruthless spree by abducting Denise Brown while she was awaiting to board a bus on Stirling Highway. Denise was their second to last victim and marked the last murder case before their cover was blown. They enticed her with a free ride after which she accepted and then held her at knife point right away.

By their fourth case, they had actually developed more skills of removing suspicions and getting away with murder. The couple forced Denise to call her parents to let them know that she was fine.

Just like with the rest of the victims, Denise was tied on the bed and raped repeatedly. This happened continuously for two days. On the following afternoon, the serial killers took their victim to Gnangara Pine Plantation. David then raped her repeatedly in the car as they awaited sunset.

At twilight, Denise was dragged from the car, a knife stabbed through her neck, while David raped her again with Catherine holding up a torch. Denise survived this, so Catherine went for a bigger knife from the car which David used to stab their victim repeatedly. When they were satisfied that their victim was dead, David dug a grave, then laid her body inside. To their bewilderment, Denise sat up gasping for air. David responded immediately by striking an axe through her head twice until she died. Denise was then buried without any other events taking place.

November 9, 1986: Kate Moir

Kate became the last victim for the sadistic serial killers and was the only one who managed to escape. She was only 17 years old when she was abducted from Stirling Highway. The Birnies spent one day torturing and raping her after which they left her in their house alone unchained the following morning. Kate had also been forced to call her parents to inform them that she was fine.

Kate had a handbag which she purposely left together with cigarettes under the bed as a proof that she had been imprisoned by the couple. Kate escaped through the window, ran half-naked to a nearby shopping centre from where she informed the police. She told the police of her suffering, and they responded immediately. On arrival at the couple's home, Catherine admitted that she recognized the 17-year-old girl but nothing apart from that. David was then brought back from his workplace in handcuffs. They told the police that Kate had not been abducted. They claimed that she came to their house by herself and all the sexual acts were performed with her consent. Both Catherine and David were arrested after the evidence of handbag and cigarettes were found

48

in their bedroom.

After a whole day of silence from the serial killers, David finally admitted to the crimes and revealed the graves of the other victims to the police. The Birnies were arraigned in court on November 12, 1986, on four murder counts, a single abduction count and rape. The perverse serial killers pled guilty on February 10, 1987, to all the charges. On the same day of their hearing, David was given life imprisonment. After a month, Catherine was given a life sentence as well but was eligible for parole in 2007.

How the Birnies' insanity came to an end

Catherine and David's sickening lives of crime came to an end on November 10, 1986. It was on Monday afternoon when people in a Fremantle supermarket, Western Australia, became startled when the half-naked Kate Moir burst in, crying that she'd been raped.

The public responded by taking her to a police station where she described that she had been held captive for a day after being dragged by a man and a woman into their car while walking in the Nedlands suburbs.

Kate narrated that she was taken to a bungalow where she was tied to the bed, then raped repeatedly by the man. The man then left the following morning for work, leaving the woman behind to watch her. She got the opportunity to escape through the window when the woman left her unchained as she went to another room.

Just after raising her alarm, the police started to question her. One of the police officers later said that he was impressed by the girl's bravery when she seized the opportunity of escaping once it appeared to her. As the girl went on recounting the story, police already were on their way headed to the Moorhouse Street white-bricked house in Willagee. Catherine Birnie answered the door. She was a hard-faced and scrawny woman. In a moment's time she and her husband were being interrogated.

David Birnie's looks were unlikely to be those of a rapist. He was slightly built with dark hair and gaunt face. He seemed too weak for him to subdue a struggling victim. When they were taken to the police station, it became apparent that there was not much fight left for them. After a day of silence, they confessed to have committed five rapes and four murders within four weeks.

Before darkness set in, the Birnies escorted the members of the Major Crimes Squad of Perth to their victims' graves. Three victims had been buried in Glen Eagle State Forest, which was about 50km to Perth's southeast. It became clear that these victims met their demise through strangling. The fourth victim was buried in a plantation and had been killed by being struck through the skull with an axe.

It was later on revealed that Catherine played a major role in their murder activities. She even took photos of the rapes performed by her husband. As the couple described their expertise in homicide, the police were left flabbergasted with the case that was way beyond their experience level – the sad narrative of a woman who enjoyed assisting her husband assault other woman. But after listening to the couple's confessions, it started to become apparent to the detectives that Catherine, the defiant woman, didn't have anything to gain from the killings; she only played her part in fulfilling the deranged lusts of her husband.

The simplicity with which the couples managed to abduct and kill their first victim is actually what paved the way to luring more victims into their treachery. After their first murder, they devised methods of attracting even more victims. They even went on to put adverts on newspaper that read "URGENT. Searching for lonely young person, preferably 18-24 years female to share a single roomed flat." This advert was found in their house after they were arrested, though it's not clear whether it bore any results like they intended.

Catherine detested one of their victims so much, to an extent of spitting on her grave when taking the police to the burying site. The victim was Noelene. David had started gaining interest in her so Catherine hated her for that. After the couple's arrest, David claimed to be remorseful for his actions, saying that he regretted deeply causing the suffering of the innocent women. It is, however, unclear whether this was genuine or just an act.

Birnie's crimes inspired much horror in the entirety of Australia. This went on to an extent that even inmates attacked him severally where he suffered injuries and had to be admitted in a hospital. When arraigned in court, the Birnies pled guilty to all charges that faced them. David claimed that he admitted to the charges so as to save the families of his victims the ordeal of prolonged court proceedings delaying his fate. The case was held on trial in the Western Australian Supreme Court on March 3, 1987. It lasted for thirty minutes only.

Brian Singleton, Catherine's attorney,

stated that she signed a statement that showed she had admitted direct involvement in each of the four murders. The lawyer said that Catherine had nothing to gain from the murders. She only took part in it just to express her complete dedication to her husband. It was all in an effort to desperately satisfy his insatiable sadistic nature.

Graeme Scoot, the Chief Prosecutor in the case of Mary Neilson, stated that it seemed as if Catherine was only interested in finding out if the victimised girl could excite her "prisoner" even more. Terry Walso, Birnie's counsel, said that his client had understood that his actions were wrong and would not present any insanity claims before the court. The belated regret expression by Birnie did nothing, however, to assist him in the case.

At last, David and Catherine Birnie were sentenced to a life imprisonment, which meant that they were to serve a 20-year minimum term in prison before gaining eligibility for parole. After the trial, Justice Wallace stated that every horrible act by the couple had been premeditated and carried out relentlessly within a very short time span. He added that Birnie shouldn't be given a chance to get out of jail forever. On their part, the Birnies never made an appeal. Catherine was confined in the Bandyup Prison in Northern Perth. David Birnie, on the other hand, was detained in the Fremantle Prison where there were several incidents with other inmates. Neither were to be eligible for parole until 2007.

4. The Snowtown Murders

The Snowtown murders happened between August 1992 and May 1999. The gruesome killing of twelve people led to the arrest and conviction of four perpetrators who were, in fact, not remorseful for many reasons. The murders led to the longest trial in Australian crime history. It was the disappearance of Elizabeth Haydon that first led to the discovery of six barrels hidden and stashed in bank vaults in a small location in Snowtown. Many books and films have been developed from the murders to document how the murders were committed.

The background

The murders were committed by three people, namely John Bunting, Robert Wagner and James Vlassakis. The police discovered the bodies in different places. However, eight of the cadavers were found in barrels that were stored in bank vaults.

Why were the murders committed? Well, most of the murders were committed as punishment. The leader of the group, John Bunting, had a strong hatred for pedophiles and homosexuals and, therefore, he killed the victims because he believed they fit into these two groups.

The perpetrators

As mentioned above, there were three people who committed these murders and later were arrested and charged. The fourth person, Mark Haydon, was not convicted of murder, but he was convicted for helping them to dispose the victims' bodies.

John Justin Bunting

Bunting loathed people who were pedophiles and homosexuals. He had this feeling due to an incident that happened to him when he was 8 years old. At this age, he was sexually assaulted by his friend's brother. As a young boy, he used to enjoy doing different things, like photography and learning about anatomy. But he lost his interests when he became an adult. When he was 22, he used to work at the slaughterhouse, and later he bragged about enjoying the feeling of dismembering the animals.

He was born in September 4, 1966, in Inala, Queensland. He lived there for a few years but later moved to Salisbury, Australia in 1991. Two of his victims were found here. He lived there for six years and later moved to Burdekin in 1997 where he stayed until 1998.

He had designed a rock spider wall which consisted of all the peoples' names he suspected to be homosexuals or pedophiles. He used to randomly choose a name from the list, call them and accuse them of being homosexuals or pedophiles. He used to threaten them by saying they deserve what is coming to them.

John married a woman named Elizabeth Harvey, but she later died of cancer. She was the mother of James Vlassakis who became a key witness in the trial. James testified that he was an accomplice and he helped the perpetrators to commit the murders. John took up the role of a father figure to James. He confided in him his hatred for the people who were homosexuals and pedophiles. During one of their conversations, James told Bunting that he was molested by his stepbrother, Troy Youde, when he was 13 years old. Bunting replied that the brother should be bashed.

Bunting and Robert Joe Wagner met in 1991 and they soon became good friends. This relationship was ironic considering the fact Wagner was a homosexual. Bunting convinced Robert to join him for committing the murders and he agreed to do that. During that time, Robert was living with Barry Lane who also helped them to dispose the body of the first victim.

An interesting fact about Bunting is that he played the *Throwing Copper*, an album by Live, produced in 1994, while he was torturing his victims before killing them.

Other perpetrators

> Robert Wagner: he directly helped Bunting in committing eleven murders.

> Mark Haydon: he assisted the duo in disposing of the bodies. He rented a building where the victims' bodies were later found in barrels. He was accused of murdering his wife and James's stepbrother named Troy Youde. The jury, however, did not find enough evidence to convict him for these murders. He was later

convicted for assisting in the disposing of the bodies.

> James Vlassakis: he also helped John to commit the murders. He helped John in torturing and killing his stepbrother who molested him. During the trial, he confessed to participating in four murders: his half-brother, David Johnson and two others.

> Elizabeth Harvey: she knew about the murders and also assisted in one of them. However, she died of cancer right after Bunting and Wagner were arrested.

> Thomas Trevilyan: he assisted in the murder of Barry Lane. But he was murdered by Bunting after he told others that Bunting was involved in the murder of Lane.

> Jodie Elliot: she was infatuated with Bunting. She was not directly involved in any of the murders, but she tried to impersonate Suzanne Elle to gain her social security benefits.

Murders

The killing spree started in 1992 and the first victim of the Snowtown murders was Clinton Trezise.

Clinton Trezise

This was the first murder that was

committed by Bunting. Clinton was 22 years old when he was murdered. John suspected him of being a pedophile and he invited him for a social visit. He later hit him violently with a shovel until he succumbed to death. He buried his body in a shallow grave. The body was discovered two years later when the investigations started.

The police did not make any connection to John at that time. In 1997, Bunting was mentioned as Australia's most wanted man and to him this was a moment of pride. He later confided to James that it was he who murdered Clinton. Bunting did not commit any murders for three years, and his next victim was Ray Davies.

Ray Davies

With the help of Robert Wagner, Bunting murdered Ray in 1995. Ray Davies was intellectually challenged. He used to live behind Suzanne's house. Suzanne was his former lover and he was accused of being a pedophile and a homosexual because he tried to take sexual advantage of Suzanne's grandsons. He was murdered but he was never reported among the missing people. However, his body was found buried in the same place as Clinton. After his death, John took possession of Ray's caravan, and he continued to receive his welfare payments.

Michael Gardiner

He was murdered in 1997 by Bunting and Wagner. He was an openly gay man and Bunting hated him for this reason. His body was found in one of the barrels that were later discovered by the police.

One of the main reasons why Bunting committed these murders was to get the welfare payments that his victims received. When he murdered Gardiner, he tried to impersonate him so that Michael's roommates would give him the necessary documents that he needed to get his funds. When his body was discovered, some parts were missing, including a leg.

Barry Lane

He too was an openly gay man. He was in a relationship with Robert Wagner, who was one of the perpetrators. The relationship began when Wagner was 13 years old; that was back in 1985 and it continued until 1996. Bunting hated Barry Lane since he believed that he was a pedophile because his relationship with Wagner had begun when he was a young boy.

On the day he was murdered, Barry was forced to call his mother and say that he wanted to break away from her and also he was leaving for Queensland. From the reports, Bunting knew that Lane was the one that assisted him in hiding Clinton's body. It was rumored that Bunting had an association with Lane, as he was helping him to learn about the pedophiles in the area. Bunting was assisted by Thomas Trevilyen.

After murdering Lane, he took ownership of his welfare payments. The body of Barry Lane was found in the same barrel of Ray Davies.

Thomas Trevilyen

Thomas Trevilyan helped in the murder of Barry Lane but he was also murdered a few days later by Bunting. The reason why he was murdered is because he told people about Bunting's involvement in the murder of Barry.

He had psychiatric problems and he used to dress only in army clothes. Bunting told the rest of the group that Thomas had become a threat and that is why he had to eliminate him. His body was found in November 5, 1997, and the police considered the death a suicide at first.

He was murdered at Kersbrook but was not dumped in the barrels like the rest of the victims.

Gavin Porter

Gavin first came into the picture in 1988 when he moved in with Vlassakis and Bunting.

He and James were friends from the time they were living in Victoria. He was not a homosexual or a pedophile, but he was addicted to heroin, and that is what angered Bunting. He was heard saying that Gavin was a waste of humanity and didn't deserve to live. What drove Bunting to the edge was a used needle that he found on the sofa. Gavin was in the car sleeping when Wagner and Bunting murdered him. His body was stored in one of the drums afterwards when they were moved to the bank vaults in Snowtown.

Troy Youde

He was murdered for revenge. He molested James when he was 13. Wagner, Bunting, James and Haydon invited Troy to visit Bunting's home. He was sleeping when they murdered him. It was reported that they tortured him before they killed him and dismembered his body. They stored his body parts in a drum before they transferred him to Snowtown.

Frederick Brookes

He was the nephew of Elizabeth Haydon and he was also the nephew of Mark Haydon. He was killed in September 1998 by Wagner, Bunting and James. They dumped his body in a car. Mark Haydon collected it and it is believed he is the one who dumped it in one of the barrels where the police found the body.

After Brookes's death Mark continued to collect Frederick's welfare payments.

Gary O'Dwayer

After a car accident that occurred early in his life, Gary became intellectually disabled. He was seen as a weak target because of his condition and also because he lived alone.

He was murdered so that Bunting could receive his payments and benefits. It is believed that he was tortured before he succumbed to his death. This is because when the police found his body, it had burn marks probably from electric shocks. His body was found with the other body in the vault.

Elizabeth Haydon

Elizabeth, the wife of Mark Haydon and the sister of Jodie Elliot, had a brief relationship with John Bunting in 1998. She was the second to last victim murdered by Wagner and Bunting simultaneously. She was murdered when Mark and Jodie were away. But Mark assisted in concealing the murder of his wife.

The following day, Garion Sinclair, Elizabeth's brother, reported her as missing. It was the report that led to the discovery of the eight other bodies. Once he reported, the police found Elizabeth's body in the vaults with the other cadavers.

After this incident, the police found enough evidence to arrest the group. They arrested Wagner, Bunting, Mark and James simultaneously.

David Johnson

This was the last murder that was performed by the group. John was the stepbrother of James, and he was lured to the bank in Snowtown. Even though he was not a homosexual, Bunting disliked him and said that he deserved to die.

Wagner and Bunting wanted to obtain his PIN and other details required for the bank withdrawal. When he arrived at the bank in Snowtown, he was cornered by Wagner and Bunting and was secured with handcuffs. They compelled him to provide the bank details and he complied. Wagner and James went to the bank in order to withdraw the money. But they were unsuccessful, and when they came back, they found David dead. Then Wagner and Bunting dismembered his body, fried it and later ate his flesh.

Susan Allen

She was involved with Ray Davies. She was murdered by Bunting and her remains were found wrapped in plastic bags. Bunting and the rest of the group claimed that she had died of a heart attack. Bunting concealed her death so that he could continue to collect her benefits. They collected $17,000 in total.

As mentioned above, Bunting had a spider wall which he used to pick his victims. The victims were randomly chosen by Bunting. The main reason why he murdered them is because he believed that they were homosexuals and pedophiles. However, this was not the only reason.

He killed other people who were obese, on drugs and intellectually disabled. Most of the victims were close friends, acquaintances and the close relatives of the members of the group. Some of the victims were befriended to collect important information before they were murdered. Most of the time, the victims' social security numbers and bank details were collected so that they could continue receiving the benefits.

Before the bodies were finally moved to the Snowtown bank vault, they were stored in different areas. They moved the body-filled barrels several times after they heard about the police involvement. There were a total of six barrels which were first stored at the house of

Bunting in 1998. Five of the barrels were stored in a Toyota Land Cruiser while the sixth barrel was stored in a Mitsubishi car. Both of these vehicles were moved to Snowtown, and later the bodies were moved to the bank vault where the police found them.

The barrels had been filled with hydrochloric acid. Because of that reason, they appeared to be mummified. As mentioned above, the murders were not carried out in Snowtown; it was the bodies that were found there. Only one victim was murdered in Snowtown, and the other victims and also the gang members were not from Snowtown.

The Capture

Even though the police had found two bodies in the woods, they could not connect all the murders. It had happened only when Elizabeth's brother reported to the police about the disappearance of his sister and then the investigations begun to take shape. The police found it odd that Mark didn't file the missing person's report, and his story was not consistent.

After discovering that Clinton and Barry Lane knew each other, the investigators began to closely study the murders and the relationship among the victims. Elizabeth's disappearance was the first clue.

67

The Trial and Verdict

The trial of both Wagner and Bunting took 12 months, thus making it the longest trial in Australian criminal history.

The first person to be convicted was James in 2001. He pled guilty to four counts of murder. He was given four life sentences, one for each murder with no parole for the first 25 years.

The Wagner and Bunting case took so long because some of the jurors fainted due to the horrific evidence that was presented in the court. After a long process, the two were eventually found guilty. Bunting was convicted of eleven counts of murder. Wagner, on the other hand, pleaded guilty to only three counts of murder but was later found guilty and convicted of seven. Each was sentenced to life imprisonment for each count of murder, without parole.

The judge presiding over the case indicated that the two killed for pleasure and, therefore, were incapable of rehabilitating. On the other hand, Mark Haydon's trial went on until 2004. He was charged with five counts of murder but he admitted to only two. He was later convicted of five counts of assisting in the murders.

Wagner and Bunting appealed their conviction but were rejected by the court. In 2005, the murder charges against Mark were dropped after he pled to two counts of assisting murders of his wife and Troy. Haydon was sentenced to 26 years in prison with no parole for the first 18 years.

The final count of the murder against Bunting and Wagner for the murder of Suzanne Allen was dropped after the jury found it hard to agree on a verdict. A lot of the information about the case was not made public because of the suppression orders of the cases.

Aftermath

After the trial and the conviction of the perpetrators, Snowtown became famous. The tourism industry of the town boosted as people wanted to visit the area. The murders, however, left a long-lasting trauma in the area. The town will forever be stigmatized because of the deaths. After the finding of the murdered bodies, the locals wanted to change the name of the town to Rosetown in order to remove the negative impact the name had. But the name change did not happen and the town still has the same name. The local stores in the area still sell different souvenirs of the crimes.

The house where Bunting used to live in

Salisbury was demolished by the owner. This is where two of the bodies were found buried. The bank with the house attached to it was auctioned but could not reach the target amount. The house was sold for $185,000 in September 2012.

Books and Films

Because of the historic impact the murders created, many books and also a film have been produced so far portraying the events of the area.

The first film was aired in 2011. Snowtown is a film that portrayed the life of John Bunting and his associates.

Different books written portray detailed information of the crimes. They include:

> *Killing for Pleasure: The Definitive Story of the Snowtown Serial Murders:* by Debi Marshall.

> *All Things Bright and Beautiful: Murder in the City of Light* by Susan Mitchell

> *Snowtown Murders; The Real Story Behind the Bodies in Barrels Killings* by Andrew McGarry

> *Snowtown: The Bodies in Barrels Murders: The Grisly Story of Australia' s Worst Serial Killings* by Jeremy Pudney

5. Eric Edgar Cooke

Background

On February 25, 1931, a child was born in a family living in Perth, Western Australia. Vivian, the father of the child, was always under the influence of alcohol and used to beat his wife, Christian, every single day. The couple was still bonded just because Christian was pregnant. The child grew up in a violent and dysfunctional family where he used to be beaten by his dad regularly. His dad used to use his hands, legs, belts and even sticks to torture the child. It took little time for the boy to realize that his father had no love for him. So he used to escape from the violent actions either by staying away from home at night or simply by hiding in the neighborhood. Who knew that the eldest of the three children of this unhappy couple, Eric Edgar Cooke, would later turn out to be one of the most feared serial killers in Australia during the '60's and would infamously be known as "The Night Caller."

Eric Edgar Cooke was born with a harelip and cleft palate. The father hated the child for such deformities. To repair the deformities, he underwent an operation when he was only three months old. He went under the knife six months later, but once again the deformities were not fully corrected. The surgeries left him with facial deformity and he could not speak clearly as well. Due to these abnormalities, he was bullied throughout his school life.

Cooke was thrown out of Subiaco State School at the mere age of six when he was caught stealing money from a teacher's purse. Then he joined Newcastle Street Infant School, High-gate Forrest Street Primary School, and Newcastle Street Junior Technical School one after the other. No matter which school he attended, he was soon expelled when they found him stealing something. Though he was good in studies and had excellent memory, he was always bullied by his school mates in every school he went to. He became ashamed of himself, lacked confidence and no matter how hard he tried, he was never able to make friends.

Eric's childhood was spent in various orphanages, foster homes and shifting schools. His dad used to buy drinks with all the money he earned, and his mother could not handle the family finances through her cleaning wages. So, in order to avoid getting bullied and to support his mother and family financially, he left school at the age of 14. He started stealing for his pocket money after he gave all the wages to his mother. Soon, stealing became his way to generate finances that helped him in making friends and impressing girls. But he was always prone to accidents wherever he worked. One day if his head was injured, the next day it would be his arms. He was hospitalized often, and the doctors concluded that the injuries occurred due to his suicidal propensities.

At 17, Eric burnt down a church because he failed in an audition for the church choir. He had to spend 18 months in jail for this misbehavior. He slowly fell into depression and frustration as nothing was going right in his life. He was psychologically affected so bad that his empty mind soon became the devil's workshop. Then the series of his crime started. He started stealing, breaking into houses and vandalizing. He was caught on March 12, 1949, for arson and vandalism at his grandmother's house. He served three years in prison for all those crimes he committed. He then joined the Australian army defying all the odds after returning from the prison. He was 21 years old when he enrolled in the army. There he trained himself how to use various weapons. But soon they discovered his past. He was then discharged from the army due to his criminal records, serving only for three months.

In October 14, 1953, Eric married Sarah Lavin, a 19-year-old waitress. Sarah was highly impressed by the big lies of Korean War that Eric told her he was a part of, and even her mother thought him as a good catch for her daughter. But the sweet dream turned into a nightmare once a child was born. The loving husband soon became a violent, cruel and angry person. The number of family members increased to nine: the couple themselves and their seven children. The couple started having a hard time meeting their financial needs. He started running into financial and emotional problems.

To get relief from them, Eric psychologically pushed and emotionally compelled to commit crimes again. He started stealing cars and breaking into houses. He was indulged in robbery and whatnot. He again got caught while stealing a car and locked behind the bars for two years this time. He was arrested many times for very trifling offences and also for being a stalker. Then he started wearing women's gloves to avoid leaving his fingerprints all over the place since he was caught due to his fingerprints in the previous crimes.

Eric was unable to get the love and care from his wife, Sarah, once the first child was born, since the compassion she had for her husband was now shared with the child as well. So he started to disrespect, beat and psychologically torture Sarah whom he used to love a lot before. He also began seeking attention from female strangers. He used to approach them in order to begin a lustful relationship. But not all the approaches were fruitful. Once he followed a woman from a bus stop and then approached her but was rejected. In order to get over the pain of rejection and get rid of all his frustration, he stole a car that very night and killed a mother of an 8-year-old boy who was cycling down the road. Thus the series of his murders began. The Australia Day rampage by him was also a result of rejection and frustration.

He was rudely told to mind his own business by a man who was having a private time with a woman late at night in a car when he noticed Cooke peeping. Cooke could not control his emotions this time as usual. Later on that day, he shot five innocent people using a rifle.

Criminal Life

In 1959, the terror of 'The Night Caller' or Eric Edgar Cooke began. He used to commit crimes in the dark of the night and hide away without leaving behind any visible evidence or witnesses. His crimes had no connections with each other, no particular patterns and there were no common traits in the victims as well. This made the police and the detectives confused since it was unlike any of the murders by serial killers they had seen. They were not even sure if there was a serial killer on the run or if these crimes were committed by several murderers. It was difficult to identify who the criminal could be, let alone catching, 'The Night Caller.'

Cooke was involved in various unrelated hit-and-run cases. He also committed crimes through shootings, stabbings and strangling. He used rifles, scissors, knives and even axes to prey upon his victims. But the rifle was his most used weapon to attack his prey and, of course the source of the knowledge of using it was the training he received in the Australian Army. Most of the victims were killed after waking up from sleep while Eric raided their homes. At one time, Cooke knocked on a door and the man who answered was killed instantly. Some of the unfortunate victims were murdered in their sleep. Once he killed his victim, raped the dead body, sexually penetrated the body with a booze bottle, and then threw the body on the neighbor's lawn. In another case, he stabbed one of his victims, then drank lemonade from the refrigerator of the victim while sitting on the veranda of the house. There was also an instance when the house owners found their pet goldfish being boiled in a pan after their home had been raided.

Patricia Berkman was the first victim of Eric. He stabbed a knife into her heart in the night of January 30, 1959. The mother lost her life and her 8-year-old son lost what could have been a happy childhood. Eric's childhood was no better, but none of that was because of Patricia or her son, Mark. The son was traumatized by the incident, so he was sent to a Melbourne orphanage as his divorced dad could not take proper care of him. Jillian Macpherson Brewer, 22; John Sturkey, 18-year-old veterinary student who was killed on Vincent Street,

Nedlands; George Walmsley, 54, a retired grocer was shot dead on Louise Street in the dawn of the day; Rosemary Anderson, 17; Brian Weir, 29; Shirley Martha McLeod, 18, who was shot in a house in Dalkeith; these are the names of some of the innocent people who lost their valuable lives due to Eric's cruelty. The number of crimes escalated, but the police could not get any leads and the criminal was still free. People were terrified every night, but the investigation was not getting anywhere.

People started questioning the efficiency of the authorities. So, they intensified their investigation. The search got more intensified when he shot five people on Australia Day; i.e., January 27, 1963. They collected the fingerprints of more than 30,000 Australian males who were above the age of twelve. In addition to this, they also started a search mission all over Australia to locate .22 rifles, and test fire them in order to identify the weapon used while committing the crimes.

In August, 1963, an elderly couple saw a hidden rifle in a bush on Rockwood Street while they were out for a walk. They notified the police and tests were conducted to confirm whether it was the rifle used for killing those victims. The forensic report confirmed the suspicion. Then an investigation team of two detectives, namely Brian Bull and Peter Skehan, devised a strategy to catch the criminal on the loose. The police replaced the actual rifle used in the crime with a similar looking rifle which was not in working condition. They stuck it in the bush tied with a cord. The place was under surveillance round-the-clock for many days. Finally after seventeen days, on a cold night in September, a vehicle stopped at 1:20 am near the spot where the rifle was found. The serial killer fell for the trap while he was trying to dig out the buried rifle. At that very moment, he was arrested by the detectives. The terror of the Night Caller finally came to an end, relieving the citizens of Australia.

Eric was overall an intelligent man and had a very sharp eye like the lens of a camera. He also had a very good memory. He could remember the events that occurred days before and things heard a long time ago like it happened just yesterday. He was known to the police due to his frequent visits to the prison for his many offences, but they never expected him to be one of the most notorious serial killers of Australia. Like most of the serial killers of all time, he was a well-groomed person, used to drive his truck and had a big family, but none of that was out of ordinary. He was often arrested for stealing, peeping and breaking into homes, but no one thought this was the guy who made the city of Perth insane. No one even thought that a person like Edgar could have a dark face like this.

After the arrest, he confessed to committing eight murders, fourteen attempted murders and breaking into more than two-hundred-and-fifty houses in Perth. As per his claim, the reasons behind these crimes were the rejections and frustrations. One of the reasons could be his dysfunctional family background or because of the way the society treated a young boy due to his deformities. Even his own dad hated him just because he was born with some deformity that he had no control over. At the crucial period of his youth, he was devoid of the love and care that every human needs. The time when a child should be playing in the arms of his father, Eric Edgar Cooke was using all his strength to save his mother from the abuse of his irresponsible, drunken father.

The bullying and hatred made a young boy into a soulless body who could no longer distinguish what was right from wrong. He chose stealing and vandalizing just to get some finances in his hands by which he could attract some friends and attention that he was hungry for. Everybody saw his outer appearance but failed to recognize the impeccable memory and learning skills of the boy. Even after many years, Eric had clear memory of when, where and how the crimes were committed. It was surprising how vividly he could recall the amount of money he stole from the victims. He trained himself to use the rifles and other weapons within just three months that he spent in the Australian Army.

The Night Caller was the reason why the Australians began locking their doors and windows before going to bed. They also began locking their cars and having pet dogs for the sake of the safety of their families and properties. Australia lost its innocence due to this man, and the initial sense of freedom was destroyed in a way that could never be restored.

When he was first considered guilty, he actually pled not guilty providing the reason of insanity. His lawyers put forth the idea of him being schizophrenic which is a kind of mental illness in order to defend him and save him from being punished. But his mental status reports proved those claims false. On November 28, 1963, the Supreme Court of Australia convicted him of eight murders and fourteen attempted murders. He could have appealed but he asked his lawyers not to do so because he thought it was his cruel behaviors that were paying him back. He spent thirteen days in New Division and on the morning of October 26, 1964, he was hanged to death in Fremantle prison when he was 33 years old. He was the last person to be hanged in West Australia, and one of the most notorious and dangerous persons that ever lived in Australia.

On the other hand, two innocent people were wrongfully convicted of murders that had been actually committed by Eric. Darryl Beamish was declared the murderer of Jillian Brewer while John Button was condemned of killing his then girlfriend, Rosemary Anderson. Though John Button had confessed to murdering his girlfriend after tough questioning by the officials, Eric confessed that he killed both Jillian and Rosemary as he swore on the Bible before he was hanged. However, he had previously denied being responsible for these two murders.

Eric Edgar Cooke is considered to be one of the most notorious criminals of all time, not only in Australia, but also in the whole world. His upbringing did not go right; neither did his schooling. He used to be physically tortured by his father and thus he was psychologically intimidated almost all the time in his childhood. Moreover, he became the victim of bullying in every school for a reason he was not responsible for, which was his facial deformities. These activities imparted a different impression on his mind. Even after his marriage, Eric was not able to feed his family well, let alone fulfill their needs. He was pushed to support his family. He tried his best to work in different places, but to his disappointment, he could not last for long on the job. He had made several suicide attempts. And one day, he took a different path and went against the law to support his family through small robbery and theft. Well, once he started committing crimes, he either could not or did not want to detach himself from it. Maybe he was addicted to it since he became an expert in committing the crimes. And he killed any person who caught him during the robberies in order to save himself. When one of the detectives who arrested him and also knew him well asked the reason behind all these crimes, he replied that the gun made him feel as if he was ten feet tall and with that he had such a rush of energy within him that he felt he could walk right through the wall.

After years of murdering people, Eric was finally caught. Well, every criminal tries to act innocent at first and Cooke was no exception. But later he confessed to all the misdoings he had done: the killing, the robbery, the vandalization, and so on. He could have appealed for his crimes for insanity or mental illness. But he did not do so as he thought he deserved punishment. After a three-day trial, he was convicted of unruly murders on November 28, 1963. He was sentenced to death by hanging by the Supreme Court of Western Australia.

In the state of Western Australia, the last person to be executed by hanging was Cooke. He had a sorrowful life and it ended in the same way. He was mentally disturbed since his childhood. The violent upbringing and his frustrating school life could possibly be the reasons behind his psychological insanity. However, he finally got what he deserved and the victims' families got justice with his demise.

6. Lindsay Robert Rose

Background

A number of notorious serial killers are there in the history of crime, and there will surely be more in the future. Most of them are known to the world for their peculiar killing habits and styles. While most of them were nabbed by the law enforcement authorities in the course of time, many had managed to stay away from the clutches of the police and any kind of punishments. Lindsay Robert Rose is an infamous Australian contract killer and serial killer from New South Wales. He wasn't as lucky as many others in his league. He was found guilty of murdering five persons in total and detained in Australia's toughest prisons. He is now serving five consecutive terms of life imprisonment without the possibility of getting a parole. Before starting his killing spree, he used to serve as a paramedic and was quite a hero in times of distress. Lindsay Rose, who committed his first homicide at the age of 29 and was Australia's most wanted criminal once, has a remarkable oddity in his character.

From one perspective, he murdered with a ruthless intensity that a therapist associated with a serious anti-social personality disorder. On the other, he was an emergency vehicle paramedic devoted to his obligation and a hero of Sydney's Granville rail disaster in 1977.

Lindsay Robert Rose was born on May 2, 1955. Throughout his childhood and adolescence period, Rose was always the kind of child who was harassed by others. Rose didn't appear to fit in anyplace, changing his jobs consistently. By the age of 29, he had attempted to be a volunteer State Emergency Services labourer, an individual from the Army Reserve and an authorized pilot trying to become a medivac. He additionally filled in as a machinist and also a private agent but was dismissed by the police in view of his poor visual perception. Rose was hailed as a legend because he was one of the main rescue officers at the time of the Granville railroad disaster. The bloodbath he saw there left him with "emotional distress." Yet, he is evidently unperturbed by his own ruthless homicides. It is strange how situations can compel people to take ruthless routes that they themselves are not aware of.

Murders Committed

On January 21, 1984, a person named Edward Cavanagh and his partner Carmelita Lee, aged 22, were gunned down in their home. Lee, who was only a casualty of situation, was secured to the quaint little bed to look on as Rose executed Cavanagh. She was then shot dead. Three years after the incident, Reynette Jill Holford, aged 46, was stabbed thirty-two times with a screwdriver because she was at her home when Rose robbed the house. This was by far the cruellest of all his murders. On February 14, 1994, massage parlour owner Kerry Pang, aged

36, and her employee Fatma Ozonal, aged 25, were shot a few times and left for dead in a blazing building. Pang, a previous partner of Rose, was shot in the right eye and cut over and over in the mid-section, neck and face by him.

On Valentine's Day of 1994, two ladies were discovered in a blazing massage parlour in Sydney. The proprietor was wounded while her representative was shot three times. It gave the idea that the owner of the parlour was the main target of this furious assault. Her husband told the police that she had been receiving threats for some time before the incident. However, he was uncertain whether it was a displeased customer or a business rival. As specialists dug into the parlour owner's recent activities, they found a lot of discrepancies. The attacker burned down the parlour in order to wipe out any proof of the incident. But the experts were still able to find the keys to a number of other murder mysteries spanning over the past decade

Lindsay Robert Rose admitted to being involved in two double murders and a single murder that was the most brutal of them all. He had an obsession of shooting and stabbing people and took pride in his good aiming. On February 14, 1994, he shot and eventually murdered Fatma Ozonal and afterward shot and cut his previous sweetheart Kerrie Pang at her massage parlour, namely "Kerrie's Oasis" in Gladesville. Ronald Waters was supposedly paid $500 to be an accomplice. His task was just to knock at the door and gain access to the inside of the massage parlour. If Waters had not knocked on the door, Kerrie would not have opened the door, thus his plan to murder her would have failed.

Her murder was orchestrated by her partner, Rose, who was later found liable for both murders and was awarded life in prison without parole for the double murder. Waters confessed to being an accomplice in this killing and was sentenced to a year and a half intermittent detainment. Waters never received the amount promised to him and he played an important role in the chain of events that unfolded the mystery behind all those murders.

Evidences at Roses' trial demonstrated that the reasons behind Pang's murder were the problems and challenges in their relationship and Rose's disappointment with Pang's profession. Fatma was never a part of the initial murder plot and was essentially in the wrong place at the wrong time. She was shot by Rose just because she was present at the scene of the crime and he feared she might have told others about the incident. Rose had earlier told the police that his relation with Pang was pretty much on the positive side and there were no problems with them. The account he gave to the officials regarding the fateful night was not accurate and had a time difference of around an hour, which was revealed during the course of investigation and by the testimonies of other key witnesses. Ronald Waters was one of the most important witnesses to the case and he helped crack two previous murder mysteries too.

Trial/Sentence

Lindsay Rose had been served with five consecutive life sentences for five murders, including the shooting and stabbing of his past girlfriend Kerrie Pang. On June 18, 1998, he confessed to committing five homicides that included those of Fatma and Pang in the Supreme Court of New South Wales. He got five consecutive terms of life imprisonment without the prospect of parole. He committed all these murders in a period of ten years, spanning from 1984 till 1994. Ronald Waters was given an eighteen month sentence while Rose was convicted for these cold-blooded murders.

Australia's Most Murderous Prison divulges that Lindsay was relocated from Supermax because of a bad case of hemorrhoids that required him to be treated somewhere else other than the prison. Lindsay used to frequently visit the little garden in the yard that is inside the Supermax facility and seemed to enjoy his stay in the prison. But he was in fact engaged in a master plan to kill a prison staff member and run away from the highly secured Long Bay Correctional Complex.

Behavioural therapist Bruce Westmore gave an insight into Rose's aggravated personality when he gave proofs amid the pre-sentencing activities. He said that he believed Lindsay Rose experienced social issues while he was growing, a condition which often influences the proficient criminals. Three of his casualties simply "happened to be there" and the other two were retribution killings, which demonstrated surprising wrath and digressed from the clean-cut homicides done by expert assassins. In any of the cases, he showed no signs of remorse; neither while killing, nor at the time of testifying.

He said, "It does suggest some personal and emotional involvements in the killings in contrast to the professional killers who seem to be detached from their victims." "There certainly seems to be an extreme instance of violence in these cases," he added.

A lot of people are unaware of his

whereabouts nowadays and are curious about his health condition. As far as we know, he is pretty much alive and will remain in the same high security prison till the day he will take his last breath. He recently seemed very concerned since a lot of prisoners in the facility are converting to Islam day by day. He even wrote a letter to the prison management on September 23, 2007, requesting a halt to the conversion of inmates. In the same year, on October 7, he smuggled letters of complaints outside the facility that mentioned the worsening conditions of the cells. The fate of Lindsay Robert Rose puts us in a position to think that you can't get away with murders and homicides, and justice prevails at the end. It is our duty to be responsible citizens after all.

AUDIOBOOKS at RJ Parker Publishing
http://rjpp.ca/ASTORE-AUDIOBOOKS

Our collection of **CRIMES CANADA** books on
Amazon.
http://bit.ly/ASTORE-CRIMESCANADA

TRUE CRIME Books by RJ Parker Publishing on
Amazon.
http://rjpp.ca/ASTORE-TRUECRIME

ACTION / FICTION Books by Bernard DeLeo on
Amazon.
http://bit.ly/ACTION-FICTION

Serial Homicide (Volume 1)
Notorious Serial Killers Series

This is the first book in the 'Serial Homicide' series which will feature six notorious cases in each volume.

Ted Bundy was a burglar, rapist, kidnapper, necrophiliac (sexual intercourse with a corpse) and serial killer in the 1970s. It's believed he killed thirty plus women.

Jeffrey Dahmer (the Milwaukee Monster), was a rapist, killer, necrophiliac, and cannibal who killed seventeen young boys and men between 1978 and 1991.

Albert Fish was a child rapist, cannibal and serial killer who operated between 1924 and 1932. It's believed that he killed at least nine children and possibly more.

During the 1980s and '90s, **Gary Ridgway** (Green River Killer), a serial killer and necrophiliac, is believed to have killed forty-nine women, but confessed to murdering seventy-one.

Between 1978 and 1983 in the United Kingdom, **Dennis Nilsen** (The Kindly Killer) is known to have killed between twelve and fifteen young men. He had a ritual of bathing and dressing the corpses, preserving them for a time before dissecting and disposing of his victims by either burning them in a fire or flushing their parts down a toilet.

Known as the Co-Ed Butcher, **Edmund Kemper** was a cannibal, necrophiliac and serial killer who, between 1964 and 1973, killed ten women including his mother who he beheaded, used her head as a dartboard and for oral sex.

Plus... Bonus Story

In February 2013, LAPD Cop **Chris Dorner** went on a shooting revenge/spree killing targeting higher-up officers and their families.

Click for *eBook* or *Paperback*

Serial Homicide (Volume 2)
Notorious Serial Killers Series

This is the second book in the 'Notorious Serial Killers' series. This volume features three male and three female serial homicide cases. **INCLUDES PHOTOS**

Included in this volume:

Between 1972 and 1978, **John Wayne Gacy** killed at least thirty-three boys and men in Illinois, of which twenty-six bodies/skeletons were buried in the crawl space under his house.

Also known as "Bind, Torture, Kill" because of his methods of killing, **Dennis Rader** killed ten people in Kansas between 1974 and 1991.

Edward Gein was a body snatcher and serial killer from Wisconsin. He would make items from corpses: lampshades made from facial skin, bowls made out of skulls, wastebaskets made from human skin.

Aileen Wuornos killed seven men in Florida between 1989 and 1990. She initially claimed that her victims had raped her while she was working as a prostitute. She later confessed that this wasn't true.

Between 1895 and 1901, **Jane Toppan**, a Nurse in Boston, killed at least thirty-one people using mixtures of drugs such as morphine and Atropine. Usually female serial killers murder for profit, Jane killed for sexual gratification.

Nannie Doss was a Black Widow serial killer who killed eleven people including four husbands, two sisters and her mother.

Click for *eBook* **or** *Paperback*

The Basement

This is a shocking story of kidnapping, rape, torture, mutilation, dismemberment, decapitation, and murder.

The subject matter in this book is graphic.

On March 24, 1987, the Philadelphia Police Department received a phone call from a woman who stated that she had been held captive for the last four months. When police officers arrived at the pay phone from which the call was made, Josefina Rivera told them that she and three other women had been held captive in a basement by a man named Gary Heidnik. He imprisoned women in chains, in the filth and stench of a hole dug under his home.

Click for *eBook* **or** *Paperback*
Also in Audiobook

About the Author

RJ Parker, Ph.D. is an award-winning and bestselling true crime author and owner of RJ Parker Publishing, Inc. He has written over 20 true crime books which are available in eBook, paperback and audiobook editions, and have sold in over 100 countries. He holds certifications in Serial Crime, Criminal Profiling and a PhD in Criminology.

To date, RJ has donated over 3,000 autographed books to allied troops serving overseas and to our wounded warriors recovering in Naval and Army hospitals all over the world. He also donates to Victims of Violent Crimes Canada.

If you are a police officer, firefighter, paramedic or serve in the military, active or retired, RJ gives his eBooks freely in appreciation for your service.

Contact Information

Author's Email:
AuthorRJParker@gmail.com

Publisher's Email:
Agent@RJParkerPublishing.com

Website:
http://m.RJPARKERPUBLISHING.com/

Twitter:
http://www.Twitter.com/realRJParker

Facebook:
https://www.facebook.com/RJParkerPublishing

Amazon Author's Page:
rjpp.ca/RJ-PARKER-BOOKS

** SIGN UP FOR OUR MONTHLY
NEWSLETTER **

http://rjpp.ca/RJ-PARKER-NEWSLETTER

Thank you to my editor, proofreaders, and cover artist for your support:

~ **RJ**

Aeternum Designs (book cover), Bettye McKee (editor), Lee Knieper Husemann, Lorrie Suzanne Phillippe, Marlene Fabregas, Darlene Horn, Ron Steed, Katherine McCarthy, Robyn MacEachern, Kathi Garcia, Linda H. Bergeron, Lynda Lata, Kali Bosworth, Tina Bates, Lorelei Pierce, Jennifer Janzen, Nancy Masterson

References

The Backpacker Murders

http://www.biography.com/people/ivan-milat-17169710#early-life

http://murderpedia.org/male.M/m/milat-ivan.htm

Arnold Sodeman

http://adb.anu.edu.au/biography/sodeman-arnold-karl-8574

https://prezi.com/wmosurzwngqe/arnold-sodeman/

The Moorhouse Murders

http://murderpedia.org/male.B/b/birnie-david.htm

http://moorhousemurder.weebly.com/crimes.html

The Snowtown Murders

http://guides.sl.nsw.gov.au/content.php?pid=242811&sid=2189491

Eric Edgar Cooke

http://murderpedia.org/male.C/c/cooke-eric-edgar.htm

http://www.crimetraveller.org/2016/08/eric-edgar-cooke-night-caller/

Lindsay Robert Rose

http://www.dailymail.co.uk/news/article 3183603/Madness-pornography-chocolate-life-REALLY-like-serial-killer-Ivan-Milat-depraved-criminals-Supermax-prison.html

http://www.austlii.edu.au/cgi-bin/sinodisp/au/cases/nsw/NSWCCA/1999/327.html

Printed in Great Britain
by Amazon